Don't Break My Nest Egg!

Don't Break My Nest Egg!

*Why Your Retirement Is at Risk
and What You Should Do About It*

David Vernich

© Copyright 2004
Revised 2005
By David Vernich

All rights reserved

ISBN: 0-9764019-0-8

Book design and layout by Charles Sutherland

*To my wonderful wife of 20 years, Connie;
and my four great sons:
Paul, Michael, Ryan, and Brad.
You five are my reason for being.*

CONTENTS

The Story
11

The Question
33

The Moral of the Story
37

Get the Upside Potential
43

The Rule of 100
47

A Brief History of Retirement
51

Show Me MY Money!
56

Running Out of Money
61

The Retirement Table of Doom
68

If You Can't Afford to Lose It
75

Don't Break My Nest egg!

The Story:

Would you buy a home on the beach without homeowner's insurance?

What if it didn't exist?

S OME TIME AGO, A NEWLY RETIRED COUPLE TOOK THEIR $100,000 nest egg and moved to Florida. They had done a good job of saving over their working years and were able to live on very little. In fact, they were able to live quite nicely on their Social Security income since they had no debt.

It had always been their dream to live on the ocean, and they finally found the perfect beachfront home. They paid cash. But this was a time before homeowner's insurance, so they had no coverage on their home. Since this type of insurance did not even exist, they thought more about the excitement of moving into their dream home than some future catastrophe that may never even happen. It had been many years since a major hurricane had hit this particular coastal town, so they felt they would be safe. Maybe if another one came, it would be long after they passed away, and then it wouldn't be their problem.

Several hurricane seasons came and went, and sure enough,

there was nothing to worry about. But as every Florida resident knows, it's not a matter of "if" but "when" the next one will come. A category 3 started spinning out in the ocean and then headed straight for their beloved community. Luckily, it wasn't a major hurricane, and the only damage it did was to take off a section of their roof. Since they had no homeowner's insurance to cover the damage, they had to pay the cost out of their own pocket. Thankfully, it was only $15,000, and they happened to have just that much money in savings.

As the roofing company was repairing the house under the watchful eyes of the owners, a car drove up with an insurance company emblem on its door. A cheerful man got out and walked over to speak with them. He had a briefcase and some papers. He informed the homeowners that due to the hurricane damage, there was some new insurance product they had invented called "homeowner's insurance." In case this ever happened again, the insurance company would pay to repair or replace the damages to their home.

"Well, how much does it cost?" was the natural response from the retired couple.

"Let me answer that question with another question," said the insurance man. "How much does your home appreciate in value each year?"

"On average?" asked the retired couple.

"Yes, on average. I know some years it goes up a lot, since there are many people moving down to retire on the beach, as you two did. And some years like this, when a hurricane rumbles through, many people want to move back to where they came from, and housing prices actually drop," observed the insurance man.

"Well, I'd say that over the time we have been here, it's probably averaged 8 percent per year," said the retired couple.

"Okay, then. Let's say the insurance company won't charge you a premium for the homeowner's insurance on a monthly basis. After all, you're a retired couple on a fixed income. I'm sure you don't want to add any new monthly bills to your tightly managed budget. But the insurance company cannot be expected to take all of the risk. Let's say that since, on average, your home appreciates 8 percent per year, the company will agree to cover only the value of your house as it appreciates up to 8 percent per year. In other words, if your home doesn't appreciate at all, you don't pay anything for this coverage. If it goes up 8 percent, you are covered for all of that gain. If it goes up by more than 8 percent, the insurance company will not cover the loss above the gain in appreciation of 8 percent per year. Then, if there is another hurricane, the company will pay the damages up to the 8 percent per year maximum so there will not be a total loss out of your pocket."

The retired couple thought for a bit, and then they responded: "We need to talk to a few people before we make such a big decision. Can we call you about our decision later?"

"Of course. But be careful not to wait too long. This is the beginning of the hurricane season, and you escaped with damages that were manageable with your savings this time, but had it been a big one, you could have lost your entire home!" the insurance agent said. He handed them a business card with his contact information, and off he went to inform the next person he could find with house damage about this new type of coverage.

The first expert the retired couple called was their real estate agent. After they explained the homeowner's insurance concept to her, they waited for her response.

"Well, I have never heard of anything like this. If it's new, it might need to be around for several years to see if it really works as they say it will. On the surface, it sounds good. But I think home prices are going to go through the roof with more and more retirees moving to Florida. House prices could escalate from 12 percent to 20 percent per year. Since you will be covered for only the appreciation up to 8 percent per year, you won't want to lose coverage on those kinds of gains to the insurance company for a loss that may never happen, do you?"

"We never thought about that. So you think the housing market is going to increase by 12 percent to 20 percent over the foreseeable future?" the retired couple asked. "Absolutely!" said the real estate agent. "That's why I advise you to forget about this homeowner's insurance, and not settle for partial coverage on all your appreciation."

The next professional they called on for advice was their accountant. He studied the brochure the insurance man had left with them and then gave his advice. "I don't think this makes much sense for someone in your situation," he said. "You folks have done a good job of living within your means; you pay cash for everything, but there is not a whole lot left after all your current living expenses. As you get older, you might need more money for health care, prescriptions, and other expenses you are not having to pay for at this time. You may potentially need to tap into your home equity to help pay for some of these expenses. I personally wouldn't want you to lose coverage on part of the appreciation gains on your home. I want you to have coverage on all your equity in case you need it down the road."

Finally, the retired couple decided to go to their banker. She had been very helpful since they moved to Florida several years ago and had steered them in the right direction with other financial issues.

After they explained to her that they had to deplete their savings account to pay for the hurricane damage to their roof, they showed her the brochure the insurance man had left them on "homeowner's insurance."

"This looks interesting," she said. "I was not aware of this protection being available."

"The insurance man told us it was brand-new," explained the retired couple.

"This might be something the bank will start requiring on all of the real estate loans we make. That way, if damages occur to houses we have liens on for mortgage loans, the insurance company will cover the loss. That will get our borrowers back to even. Right now, I have a list of homeowners who want to see me to get a loan to cover the damages the hurricane caused. Not everyone has managed to save and pay cash for the needed repairs as you two did," commented the banker.

"Since you don't have a mortgage on your house, it is entirely up to you. The bank can't require you to have coverage, since we don't have a lien on your home. We would probably make it a condition on any new money we lent to anyone, because banks don't want to take a risk that can be transferred to an insurance company for a reasonable price. Now we are looking at hundreds of loan requests on damaged homes that people will be paying off for years."

The retired couple left the bank and went home to discuss their options. Although the experience with the recent hurricane was bad, they were able to handle it. They figured that if a hurricane such as this happened every ten years, they would have to save $1,500 per year to get back the $15,000 they had spent on repairing their roof.

On the other hand, if their home appreciated 20 percent per year, that would be $20,000 worth of appreciation. If they took the insurance company up on their offer, they would be covered for only $8,000 of that. That would leave $12,000 that would not be a covered loss, which was way more than the $1,500 per year they would have to save to replenish their savings account.

"Let's not take the insurance," the retired couple decided. "The real estate agent was against it, the CPA advised us not to, and the banker left the decision up to us. After looking at the math, I think the answer is obvious."

A couple of days later, the insurance man stopped by. He was on his way to write a homeowner's insurance policy for their next-door neighbor, who had suffered a loss equal to theirs.

"Did you two have a chance to look over the information I left

Why Your Retirement Is at Risk

you, and do you have any questions I can answer for you?" the insurance man asked.

"We did, and after talking to our advisers and discussing it between ourselves, we've decided not to take this insurance coverage," the retired couple responded.

"I'm surprised you were advised not to take this coverage. May I inquire as to the reasons why?" the insurance man politely asked.

"Well we really don't want to get into any confrontation about our decision. We feel it's just not the right thing for us. But you have not been pushy, so we'll tell you how we came to our decision. Our real estate agent said that our home should appreciate between 12 percent and 20 percent per year. Giving up coverage on those gains over 8 percent could mean a lot of money out of our pocket down the road. Our CPA said we would need this money in the future for expenses that we might have as we get older. And our banker actually liked the product, but said it may not be necessary for us, since we don't have a mortgage against our house. We did the math, and we think we are better off saving $1,500 per year to replenish our savings versus potentially losing coverage on a big chunk of our home's appreciation," the retired couple responded.

"I respect your decision and will not try to change your mind. Before I leave, though, let me make an observation regarding the advice you received. Your real estate agent is selling you on the idea that your home is going to appreciate 20 percent per year. Although that may happen, it won't happen every year. So why don't you ask her if she will guarantee that it will go up by 12 percent per year in writing? I know she won't. So the fact that you're basing your decision on what might or might not happen in the future should be something to consider," the insurance man commented.

"The CPA might be right about your expenses going up as you get older, but he won't guarantee that a hurricane won't come next year and demolish your home. If that happened, your expenses would go up dramatically to repair the damages, and you may not be able to get a bank loan if the damages exceed your savings and your income is not enough to justify the monthly loan payments."

The insurance man got up to leave. "You may want to consider what your banker said. After all, your home is your largest asset, and to leave it unprotected based on the advice of professionals who won't stand behind their 'guarantee' of what might or might not happen in the future is a little bit shaky. I hope you know what you are doing. Good luck." And with that, the insurance man left.

As the retired couple thought about what the insurance man had said, they felt sure of themselves. They had done their homework and made an objective comparison. This was something they felt strongly about not doing. And with that, they went on with their lives as if they had never been introduced to "homeowner's insurance."

Time went on and there were no more hurricanes to contend with for the balance of the year. The next year went by without incident as well. The retired couple's savings account was beginning to be replenished after taking all of the money to pay for roof repairs resulting from the hurricane two years ago.

Inflation was beginning to kick in, and they were having a harder time keeping up on a fixed income. Unexpected expenses for health care were becoming a more frequent event, and it was becoming difficult to fully fund their savings account as they had originally planned.

The good news was that their beachfront house had gone up in value every year. Over the past five years, they estimated it had appreciated almost 12 percent per year on average. But that appreciation did nothing to help them with their problem at hand. Their monthly expenses were rising faster than their income, and they needed to look for ways to increase their income.

Since their home was their largest asset, they decided to start there. They had lived in this house for several years and, except for the one mishap with the hurricane, it had been a pleasant and profitable experience. They did some research and found that the area they had moved to was experiencing a huge influx of people wanting to live a similar lifestyle. Oceanfront real estate was at an all-time high, and the demand for it had outstripped the supply.

After careful consideration, the retired couple decided to build an addition onto their house so they could rent it out to snowbirds for some income. They felt that they could handle another retired couple living next to them in a duplex-type apartment. The extra income would really take some pressure off their budget, and they might enjoy the company of a couple their age.

There was only one problem. They didn't have the cash to do the addition. So they typed up a proposal with construction estimates and a projected profit-and-loss statement on the rental income versus the anticipated monthly payment on a loan and went to their banker for advice.

DON'T BREAK MY NEST EGG

"Long time no see!" their banker responded when they walked into her office. "How have you been?"

"Pretty good," replied the retired couple. "We've been enjoying our home and the weather."

"What can I do for you today?" asked the banker.

"We would like to apply for a loan. Our expenses have finally caught up with our income, and we don't want to wait until it becomes a larger problem before we do something about it."

"I like to see people who are proactive about their finances," the banker commented. "What are you planning to do?"

"We have a proposal here for an addition to our home so we can rent it out and have it produce some additional income for us," came the retired couple's reply. "Our request is for $100,000."

"Based on what I know of your credit history and the equity you currently have in your house, that should be no problem. I think it is a wise move for you to take this on now before your expenses rise above your income level. That would make it more difficult for us to approve a loan for you," the banker commented.

"By the way, what did you two ever decide to do about that homeowner's insurance you came to talk to me about several years ago?" asked the banker.

"We decided not to get it," came their reply.

"Oh, really? And why not, may I ask?"

"Our real estate agent and CPA said we really didn't need it. Besides, our home has appreciated dramatically, and the insurance company would not have even covered us fully on all of the gain," the retired couple proudly answered.

Why Your Retirement Is at Risk

"Well I hope you realize that the bank has taken the stance that it will not lend money to anyone for real estate unless they purchase homeowner's insurance. The bank does not want to take on the risk of damage to the property from a hurricane unless they are assured that the money to fix the home will be there from a strong insurance company. The only exception to this rule is for people who have enough cash to fully pay the cost of replacing their home," the banker explained.

"Oh, dear. That wouldn't be us, then. So we have to take out this homeowner's insurance as a condition to the bank's making a loan to us?" they asked.

"Yes, that is correct," the banker answered. "I can put you in touch with an agent we have found to be extremely knowledgeable about this coverage."

So the retired couple took down the information and went back home. It turns out that the person they were referred to was the same insurance man who had come to their home after the hurricane had hit. He came over one afternoon and met with the retired couple for a second time.

"Hello, strangers!" the insurance man cheerfully exclaimed as he recognized the couple from his talk with them several years ago. "I'm kind of surprised to see you two again!"

"We are, too," replied the couple. "But we were left with no choice, since our banker said that we needed to get some coverage if we were going to get a loan from them."

"So you didn't change your mind from our first meeting?" the insurance man responded.

"No, in fact, we're glad we didn't take out the coverage because we never would have used it," the retired couple proudly related.

"I understand that," came back the insurance man, "but you could say the same thing about your car and life insurance, and you still have those."

"Right now, we have no choice but to look into this coverage again because it is a condition of getting a loan from the bank. Can you tell us if the product has made any changes since the last time we spoke?" inquired the retired couple.

"After the last hurricane, we had an explosive demand for this coverage. There is nothing like the painful sting of a major loss to get people to think about how they could avoid having to go through that experience again. And banks were our major promoter. They could not stand to see so many people turned down for loan requests to fix their homes because they did not have enough income to make the monthly loan payments. There is nothing worse than having to foreclose on someone's house that is damaged, pour in more money to fix it up, and then resell it to someone else to get the bank's money back," the insurance man quietly explained.

He continued. "Actually, there have been some enhancements to the product since we last spoke. It was specifically designed for people such as you who are still putting money into a house in the form of monthly payments. Now, in addition to the insurance company's guaranteeing that you will not suffer a complete loss due to a hurricane or other disaster, they will match your monthly payments with ten cents for every dollar."

Why Your Retirement Is at Risk

"For example, let's say your monthly mortgage payment is $500. The $500 monthly payment you make to the bank will be matched by the insurance company with $50. So your equity builds by 10 percent every time you make a payment!"

"Well, how much does that cost us? The insurance company certainly doesn't do that for free!" the retired couple skeptically responded.

"You're right, the company doesn't do it for free. However, the original pricing that I explained to you during our first meeting is still the same. Once again, the company covers only the gains on the appreciation of your house up to 8 percent per year. So you are covered for all the appreciation up to 8 percent. If your house does not appreciate by more than 8 percent, then your coverage is basically free," the insurance man explained.

"But our home has appreciated more than 8 percent over the past several years," the retired couple objected. "We would have given up coverage on a large part of the gains if we had taken out the insurance when you originally showed it to us."

"How much, on average, do you think your home has appreciated since we last met?" came the insurance man's immediate reply.

"We have been told 12 percent from a variety of sources," the retired couple quickly responded.

"Okay, then. If that is true, you would have given up coverage on 4 percent of the gains on your house. Your house was originally worth $100,000, so that means the insurance company would not have covered $4,000 on average per year in appreciation over this time period. But you must take into consideration that homes

DON'T BREAK MY NEST EGG

don't go up by 12 percent per year forever, and that this will even out, with some years at or below 8 percent, which will cost you nothing in those years. Also, if there had been a major hurricane that damaged your home, would you have had the cash to make the repairs?" came the insurance man's rebuttal.

The retired couple were unfazed. "We could play these what-if scenarios all day long. We still stand by our original decision not to take the coverage and, in retrospect, we're happy with that decision today. Now, about our immediate need: How can we take care of what the bank wants without giving up coverage on 100 percent of our appreciation?" inquired the retired couple.

"The only way to accomplish both of your goals is to build a separate building that we can insure for the bank, and then we won't have to put coverage on your current home," the insurance man said.

"Now that sounds like a good compromise. We can leave our current house the way it is, and take coverage on only the new rental house to keep the bank happy so they will give us a loan. That should work! Let's do it!" the retired couple exclaimed.

The bank went along with their decision and made the loan for the rental house. Since they had just enough land for two small homes, it seemed the perfect compromise. So the rental was built, advertised, and rented out fairly quickly due to the high demand from incoming retirees and snowbirds. Everything was going exactly as planned.

Several years went by after the completion of their rental house. The retired couple continued to make their mortgage payment of $500 per month, and they were excited to see that the insurance company was kicking in their 10 percent on each payment, which meant their equity was increasing at a faster rate.

However, they were still disappointed that they had to have the insurance when they were seeing home prices climb ever higher. They had been at the right place at the right time for the first time in their lives, and their home and rental property were appreciating just as their real estate broker had predicted. And it seemed there was no end in sight. The demographics of the population in the U.S. were getting closer and closer to retirement age, and more and more people were moving to Florida to take advantage of the sunny, warm weather.

By this time, they were stunned to find out after a call from their real estate professional that their home itself was probably worth $1 million in today's booming market! Their original investment had increased ten times. They were smug after this phone call, and started to feel that they had made all the right financial moves. They thought to themselves, "Luckily, we didn't give in and get homeowner's insurance from that insurance man when he first came to us. Now we have a paid-for $1 million house!"

There had not been a hurricane since the one many years ago that caused $15,000 in damage, and another hurricane season was fast approaching. Sure enough, this was the year a hurricane was identified many hundreds of miles away that was heading in the general direction of Florida.

Housing prices in the retired couple's area had leveled off after several hot years of double-digit growth, and the last few years had actually gone flat or well below the 8 percent average. The cooling off of the real estate market and the appearance of a threatening hurricane made the retired couple think.

"Maybe we should look into getting that homeowner's insurance again," they pondered. "It really has worked out well for the rental house, with that 10 percent credit for our payments as a nice added bonus. And we really haven't given up much on the appreciation side, either. The rental has appreciated most of the time at 8 percent or less, so we really did not give up much coverage on the full appreicated value of the house," they reflected.

So they made the call to the insurance man. "Sorry," came the apology from the insurance man. "The insurance company has suspended the sale of homeowner's insurance in the area until after the hurricane season," he said. "The company will not take the extra risk with a hurricane brewing. It is always hard to get coverage when you really need it." And with that, the call was over.

As they pulled into their driveway, the couple noticed their renters packing their car. "The weatherman said it would be a good idea to evacuate before the rush, so we're heading back north," the renters explained. "From the satellite photos, it looks like the hurricane is coming in this direction."

The retired couple were stunned. It had been years since a hurricane had come through this area, and just when things were going so smoothly, with their two houses going up in value, this happens! Now the worry began to set in.

"What will we do if the hurricane comes here?" they asked each other, already knowing the answer. Soon enough, they would be

Why Your Retirement Is at Risk

able to see for themselves. So they packed up and evacuated like everyone else, not knowing what to expect when they returned to their beloved home.

It was the hurricane season of 2004, when three different hurricanes crisscrossed Florida and wreaked havoc on a scale that had not been seen in decades. Little did the retired couple anticipate when they left their beachfront home that it would be more than six weeks before they could return to see for themselves the damage inflicted on their property.

When they finally did arrive back home, nothing could have prepared them emotionally for what they saw. The hurricanes had lived up to their hype, and the damage was massive. The retired couple's two beachfront homes were gone. Only parts of the foundation were indicators of where the houses once stood. It was a total loss.

Soon, a car pulled up with a familiar insurance company emblem on its door. They knew who this was and what he was there for. It was their insurance man, and he soberly approached the retired couple, who were still in shock.

"Hello, folks. I'm glad to see you're okay. It's hard to fathom, isn't it?" He paused for a moment to gather his thoughts. "As you know, you have coverage on the rental house, and we will be cutting a check to you and the bank for its full value. You will be able to rebuild that structure, and it will be as if this hurricane had never occurred."

The insurance man continued. "Unfortunately, you decided against having coverage on your home, so that loss will be fully your responsibility. The insurance company will have the check to the bank for your rental house by the end of the week. I'm truly sorry for your loss." And with that, the insurance man was off to take care of other clients to whom he had sold homeowner's insurance.

"Well, at least he didn't gloat or tell us he told us so," said the retired couple to each other. "A $1 million house is gone! We don't even have a fraction of that kind of money to rebuild. What have we done?" They wanted to retrace the steps that had brought them to this point.

"We spoke to our real estate broker, and she had us convinced that to give up coverage on some of our real estate gains was foolish. And we were greedy! We wanted it all. We got it all, too. All of the gains and all of the losses! What good did all that appreciation do us, since it has evaporated before our very eyes? All of those gains were ours to keep only if we sold the house and cashed out all our equity, or at the least, had it insured for most of its ever-increasing value so if a loss like this did occur, we would at least have gotten back to where we were before the storm.

"The gains in our home's value were merely 'phantom gains.' Sure, the real estate market went up more than 8 percent per year on many occasions. And we thought those gains were 100 percent ours to keep. But what good is it to see supersized gains year after year if when everything is said and done, we walk away with nothing? If we had been happy with an 8 percent average gain on our homes, we would have at least kept that.

"Our CPA also led us in the wrong direction. Where is all this equity in our homes that we're supposed to have for our later years? It's gone! And we are the ones who are going to suffer for taking their advice. They are going to be back practicing their professions, making money on selling real estate and preparing taxes, and we are the ones who are taking the hit. They did not guarantee any of their advice, nor did they suffer one bit from giving us incomplete information. We were responsible for taking their advice, and now we are going to have to live with this decision for the rest of our lives."

Later in the week, they went to their bank. "I have a check from the insurance company made out jointly to the two of you and the bank. We can use the money to rebuild your rental house or, if you choose, we can pay off the balance of the loan and you can keep the cash that's left. If you decide not to rebuild on your land, you can sell off the beachfront property and, together with the remaining insurance money, you should be able to afford a modest home anywhere in the country," the banker said.

"A modest home?" thought the retired couple. "What happened to our $1million home?" It was gone and they were devastated. It was too late for them to start all over, even with a paid-for piece of land. It had taken years and years to build up that kind of value, and it was destroyed in an instant.

"At least you have something to show for all your years," the banker said to try to comfort them. "It would have been a total loss if not for the homeowner's coverage on the rental house. If you look around, there are a lot of people who had no coverage at all who would gladly switch places with you. They are going to live with the consequences of having no coverage for the rest of their lives. It's too bad, too. It was all avoidable."

With that, the retired couple got in their car and headed north, far away from the effects of hurricanes and thankful they weren't destitute like many of the people who had all their salvaged belongings in tow. They would have many years to mull over the day when they were introduced to "homeowner's insurance" and didn't fully take advantage of it.

"A $1 million paid-for home. Gone in an instant. Why didn't we protect our largest asset when we had the chance?" The question haunts them constantly to this day.

The Question:

Now for a question posed to you . . .

WHAT WOULD YOU HAVE DONE HAD YOU BEEN THE RETIRED couple at the beginning of this story? Hindsight is always 20/20, and it is a lot easier to see what should have been done after the fact. Anyone would have chosen to get homeowner's insurance if they knew their house was about to be destroyed. But after a period of several years of relative calm, and before it was inevitable that the storm was coming in their direction, the decision may have not been so clear-cut.

So, before reading on, stop and put some serious thought into your response to that question. Once you have firmly answered the question in your own mind and for your own circumstances, read on.

The Moral of the Story

SOMETIMES IT IS EASIER FOR US TO FORMULATE AN OPINION ON A matter when it happens to somebody else. We get too used to doing things our own way, and we carry preconceived baggage that makes us unable to see the forest for the trees. This is something that happens to everyone, and until we can look at a situation from a variety of angles, the correct decision may never become clear.

In the story about the retired couple, this is something we all can identify with and maybe even see ourselves doing at some point in our lives. The exact timetable is unclear, but the facts of this case are believable and realistic.

We all are the "retired couple." In the story, Florida represents the stock market. If you are in the stock market, which most of us are, then you put yourself in jeopardy due to hurricanes, or market corrections. Since most people keep their retirement assets in financial vehicles such as 401(k)s, IRAs, individual stocks, and mutual funds, we all are living in Florida with our largest single asset unprotected: our retirement nest eggs.

For the first time, a new financial product has been introduced to take care of the devastating risk of loss to our retirement assets. Like homeowner's insurance, it protects a substantial asset from a devastating loss. We like to call it "nest egg insurance." Unfortunately, most people are unaware that this protection exists. There are several reasons for this.

One, it is relatively new and like anything new, it has not gained widespread popularity. There has not been a lot written about it in the financial press, nor will you see it advertised in most mass media publications. But this is not the main reason you probably have never heard of this coverage. The industry that is supposed to be selling it—the financial professionals in this country, of which there are thousands upon thousands—are not promoting it to the extent they should.

Why not? Because most of these "financial advisers" would rather sell what is popular and go along with the herd than take an objective look at something that could save their clients from having to risk their "homes" every "hurricane season." They would rather you focus your attention on the market and repeat the same old advice: "On average the market will give you a return of 10 percent to 12 percent per year" (which the financial adviser will never guarantee in writing).

Also, if the financial adviser (or real estate broker in the story) had you move some of your retirement assets under this protection, he or she would lose control of managing those assets. You see, they get paid a commission when securities are bought *or* sold, regardless of whether *you* are making money or losing money. So

Why Your Retirement Is at Risk

many of these advisers will not suggest you acquire "nest egg insurance," because that could mean money out of their pocket.

If you have ever unexpectedly lost money in retirement accounts managed by someone you pay, and you were shocked to see a decline in the value of your assets, you need to fire your financial adviser. Either they did not do a good job explaining the risks of investing in the market, or they did not position your assets properly to avoid the loss. Either way, they didn't do their job of safeguarding your money and need to feel the pain of losing your business.

In every prospectus for the sale of securities there are always two phrases, which you may not have paid much attention to:

1. Past performance is no guarantee of future results.
2. Account may lose value; not FDIC-insured.

And yet very little time is spent with the individual investor discussing the ramifications of these two statements. Instead, "financial advisers" parrot the industry mantra: "On average, the market goes up (8 percent to 12 percent) per year." And when the market is falling: "Dollar cost averaging will allow you to buy more shares at a lower price so that when the market rebounds, you will be better off."

Historical averages don't mean anything to you as an individual investor unless you have access to a time machine and can go back, invest in those particular stocks or mutual funds with the great historical returns, and capture all those gains.

It's a lot like trying to drive a car by looking only in the rearview mirror. That is why most financial advisers are usually fond of saying: "Objects (financial returns) in the mirror are closer than they appear." Especially when the car is driven into a ditch because the driver was paying attention to what has already happened in the past instead of paying attention to what is coming up on the road ahead.

So what is the answer to this problem? Insure the portion of your retirement assets you cannot afford to lose, just as you insure your home against fire or storm damage. Why take unnecessary risk, especially when a strong insurer will do it for you and pay you for the right to insure your nest egg! How is this possible?

Like our example with the retired couple, if you were to look at having your retirement nest egg insured, the insurance company would pay you a bonus of 10 percent for all assets you want covered. If you had $100,000 to insure, the insurance company would immediately credit you with $110,000 ($100,000 of your own money plus $10,000 for the bonus)! Where else would a financial company give you this kind of deal?

And, like the retired couple, you choose how much of your nest egg you want insured. If you want to invest in the market with a portion of your retirement assets, that is completely in your control. You get 100 percent of the gains and 100 percent of the losses, just as in the story.

But rather than have all your money at risk all of the time, you now have another option:

Get the Upside Potential of the Market Without the Downside Risk!

That's right! Finally, a financial product that lets you keep what you have contributed and earned, so that you never have to worry about the market crashing at age sixty-four when you're ready to retire and losing half or more of what you've accumulated during forty-plus years of hard work. It just doesn't make much sense, does it?

The two great industries that stand to lose the most from the wide acceptance of this product are the banks (with money tied up in low-yielding, taxable CDs) and the stock brokerage and mutual fund companies (with retirement savings tied up in the high-risk stock market). There is a place for both of these institutions in regard to your personal finances.

However, the problem is that these industries have no incentive to tell you about nest egg insurance. If they do, they stand to lose control of your money. Money you have put with them that they need to lend out or invest so they might make a return for themselves. I am not against either of these institutions. But there are

DON'T BREAK MY NEST EGG

billions and billions of dollars that are not in the proper place and need to be insured against loss.

Banks are great for short-term deposits that you will need to get your hands on in five or fewer years. This includes checking accounts, money market accounts, savings accounts, and CDs. For retirement purposes, banks are a terrible place to keep your money! Why? Because the return on your money is mediocre at best, and the interest you earn every year is taxable! Yuck! But that is the price you pay to keep your money liquid. And banks are fine for that portion of your money.

Mutual funds and stocks are great places for investments, but not with money you cannot afford to lose. The trouble is, most stock jockeys will tell you that you need to put as much money as you can into the stock market because, long term, that is where you will get the greatest return. I don't argue with that point except for one small difference: *Do not put any money in the market that you cannot afford to lose!*

So render unto banks the money that belongs in banks, and render unto brokerage firms the money that belongs at risk of loss in stocks. But a lot of money out there doesn't belong in either and needs to be insured for a secure retirement. And for that reason, banks and brokerages will fight tooth and nail to not lose your business! How do you decide how much of your money should be insured?

The Rule of 100

A LITTLE COMMON SENSE WILL WORK JUST FINE. MOST FINANcial advisers tell people they need to become more conservative the closer they get to retirement. They use something called the "Rule of 100." The simplest explanation of the "Rule of 100" is that your age is the percentage of your retirement assets that should be kept in something that cannot lose money. For example, if you are forty years of age, then 40 percent of your retirement assets should have "nest egg insurance," and the remaining 60 percent (100 − 40 = 60) could be in the stock market at risk. The theory behind this is that as you get older, the less time you have until retirement and the less time you have to recover from a market correction (hurricane).

This is only a rule of thumb. If you are more of a risk taker, or plan to delay your retirement by working longer, you can increase the percentages to better reflect your personal comfort level of risk. However, most people would do good to stick close to these percentages, because their risk-tolerance levels are a lot lower than they think. All it takes is one massive market correction to tell you if you made the right decision on your percentages.

For example, it is a lot easier to take a 50 percent decline on 60 percent of your assets than a 50 percent decline on 100 percent of your assets. Let's say you've done a terrific job and have accumulated $1 million in retirement accounts. If you had nest egg insurance on 60 percent of your retirement savings (or $600,000) and had 40 percent at risk in the market for the potential of higher returns (or $400,000) and the market drops by 50 percent, you would have lost only $200,000 (still a painful number) instead of $500,000 had you not insured your nest egg at all.

A Brief History of Retirement

TO UNDERSTAND THE PRESENT STATE OF RETIREMENT ISSUES, WE must first go back and understand the history of retirement as a concept itself. Prior to World War II, people did not retire to a life of leisure at age sixty-five. They worked until they could no longer work, and then their families took care of them until they died. People did not tend to live very long back then, because of a lifetime of hard labor and a healthcare system still in its infancy. The average age at death back then was sixty-seven! Not a very long retirement, indeed. In fact, much of the world operates with this same "retirement system" today.

The Social Security system was not established until 1935 by President Franklin D. Roosevelt. America was primarily an industrial society with a large portion of its workforce laboring in factories and steel mills. We were a blue-collar society and work was physically demanding; so much so that by the time someone was close to sixty-five years old, they could not physically do the work required of them.

Luckily, employers and the federal government came to the conclusion that people should be afforded "retirement" as a reward for employees' loyalty and long years of service. Not to mention there were millions of baby boomers about to come into the job market and they needed to move people out (sixty-five-year-olds) so they could move in. Pensions (which would pay a percentage of ones' salary after retirement) were put into place, and generous healthcare benefits were also promised so that retirees would have no worries financially.

With the combination of federal government programs like Social Security and company provided pensions and health care, people could finally "retire." The success of these plans would be short-lived, though. Basically, only one generation would live to see the combined programs work as they were intended.

In 1974, President Gerald Ford signed into law something called ERISA ("Employee Retirement Income Security Act"), which was largely ignored by the American public. They did not understand that what had happened was a seismic shift from employers being responsible for their employees retirement security to each person being responsible for their own retirement security.

Unfortunately, the passage of the law did not give the public notice of this major change in policy. Since corporations were still offering pensions and health care to their employees and Social Security was still supposed to pay benefits in addition to Medicare, people were lulled into a false sense of security about their retirement.

Pensions are *defined benefit* plans, meaning the company defines how much of a benefit you will receive in retirement based on a formula the company determines using an employee's salary and years of service. For example, if someone retires after thirty years of service with an average salary of $40,000 during those thirty years, the company will continue to pay the employee, say, $25,000 per year. When coupled with Social Security benefits, people had enough money coming in that they didn't need to work any longer.

ERISA made the change to *defined contribution* plans possible. This meant that your income in retirement was entirely up to you because you had your own personal account set up, called a 401(k). *If* you contributed (it was voluntary, so you didn't have to), and *if* you contributed enough (you decided how much to put in), and *if* you chose the proper investment vehicles that would drive the return on your money (because you were responsible for choosing between multiple investment options), then you could potentially have an even greater retirement income than the previous generation, which had only their pensions and Social Security benefits to live on. But there were a lot of "ifs" that had to work out properly in order for this to happen.

Conversely, if one did not do all of these things, you would find yourself destitute at age sixty-five with no other option but to continue to work (*if* you could find work), or live a meager existence on Social Security (which was never meant to be the sole source of retirement income for an individual), or become a welfare case for the government or family to support. Not attractive alternatives for either party (when was the last time you chose to go out and eat at a federal government subsidized school cafeteria?).

In the late 1990s, we all experienced that "irrational exuberance" that popped our pipe dreams of early retirement. Prior to that event, we were all stock market gurus who could double our money every year or two. To paraphrase Warren Buffett, until the tide goes out, we really don't know who is swimming without a swimsuit! And we never even had to read one entire prospectus or take a single class in economics, business, or finance! What a deal!

We're all a little wiser now, but the fundamental problem still hasn't changed. Today, like it or not, the government and employers are shifting more and more of the burden of our retirements into our laps. Either we can choose to ignore it and take our chances when we reach retirement age, or we can take the bull by the horns and try to figure out how things work so that we don't join the long and dismal chorus of people in the former group.

History is replete with examples of people and entire countries that have chosen to take the easy road today, only to find that the road gets infinitely more difficult as time passes, with fewer options and virtually no hope for a better future. Taking the harder road today, when many of the people you encounter refuse to acknowledge that there is even a problem, will pay huge dividends in the future. After all, Noah started to build the ark 120 years before the Flood came!

Show Me MY Money!

Since the market crash of 2000, I have spoken to many disillusioned investors and financial professionals. I've heard stories from financial advisers about people who were disappointed with a 34 percent return on their money when they read stories in the paper about people who had put money into dot-com stocks and were seeing 100 percent–plus returns and would call and move all their money to another financial adviser. It was a time of greed and stupidity, but hindsight is always 20/20.

Fortune magazine recently interviewed several top money managers, proving this quote has always been true: "People have an infinite risk tolerance when they are making money and a zero risk tolerance when they are losing money." Trillions of dollars of assets were wiped out in retirement accounts in this country because simple precautions were not followed. In fact, baby boomers have lost $5 trillion in retirement assets (approximately 30 percent) since the spring of 2000!

DON'T BREAK MY NEST EGG

People had all their nest eggs tied up in retirement accounts that had no ceiling (there was no limit to how much they could earn on their investments) but also had no floor (in theory, they could lose 100 percent of their money along with their returns). And there were many more who suffered a worse fate when they bought into their companies' lies and chose to put all their retirement nest eggs in their company stock. Enron, Worldcom, Tyco, Bethlehem Steel, United Airlines, and many more companies stock have fallen off a cliff and have taken their employees' retirement security with them.

So tell me, how is the average person supposed to have any chance in a system where their retirement money is turned over to a professional money management firm that works full-time tracking company stocks with MBA analysts and whose company financial statements are audited by full-time professional CPAs and whose numbers are pored over, analyzed, and scrutinized by teams of full-time professionals and the Securities and Exchange Commission, and yet NONE OF THEM were able to catch people who were driving billions of dollars out the back door of the companies they ran into the ground until it was too late?

The answer is quite simple. The reason people chose to ignore these problems was because, at the time, their retirement statements were showing a positive return! Once the problems were realized and the market reacted, the people who were previously happy with their returns saw their account balances drop like a rock, with no ability to exit before it hit the bottom! So much for those years of double-digit gains.

You see, the only way you can calculate the true rate of return on

Why Your Retirement Is at Risk

an investment is to put money in, wait some period of time, and take all the money out. Then you can see if you had a gain or a loss, and calculate how much (the percentage). Otherwise, all you have is funny money. It's not yours to keep until you take it out of the market. But we sure act as if it's ours when we see it on our statements, and we feel the pain as if it's ours when we see it disappear from our account balance.

Aesop's Fables are timeless classics, stories that have relevance over thousands of years because human nature does not change that much. We can all remember the story of the tortoise and the hare, and investment returns in retirement accounts are a good analogy we can apply to this story. People who take on higher risk with faster growing stocks than those who take a slower, safer, and more steady approach may finish the race last (or not at all). As Mark Twain said, as he got older he was more concerned with "the return *of* my money than the return *on* my money."

What most people don't realize is that it can take a long time to recover from an aggressive retirement investment strategy if the market turns against you. On the next page is a chart showing three variables. The first is a hypothetical percentage loss in market value for your nest egg. The second is the subsequent percentage gain thereafter. And the third is the amount of time it takes for you to get back to even. The only variable it doesn't show that is extremely important to you individually is: At what age does this happen to you? In other words, if this happens to you just prior to retirement, it's time for you to get a job application as a Wal-Mart greeter. If it happens to you early on, you might have time to recover. But was the ride up worth the fall down?

DON'T BREAK MY NEST EGG

Hypothetical Loss in Nest Egg Value	Hypothetical Gain Thereafter @		
	+ 3%	+ 6%	+ 8%
@ 10%	3.6 years	1.8 years	1.3 years = How long it will take to get back to even!
@ 20%	7.5 years	3.7 years	2.9 years =
@ 30%	12 years	6 years	4.6 years =
@ 40%	17 years	8.6 years	6.6 years =
@ 50%	23.2 years	11.6 years	9 years =

During the Great Depression in 1929 when the stock market crashed, the market fell 88 percent before it hit bottom. It was not until 1954 that the market recovered to its high in 1929! That took 25 years!

In more modern times, the worst bear market since the Great Depression (excluding the crash of 2000–2002 since, as of this date, we have not fully recovered) was 1973–1974 which took seven years and six months to regain the previous market high point. So, if you had purchased an S&P 500 index fund at the end of 1972, it would still be 9 percent below where you purchased it at the end of 1979!

Running Out of Money Before You Run Out of Time

A MERICANS HAVE, BY AND LARGE, TOTALLY ABDICATED THE responsibility of managing their investments to "professionals." And that is fine if: (a) you don't want to spend the time to educate yourself on investments and how they work or, (b) you are willing to take whatever the results are if the people, whom you probably will never meet but have been entrusted with your money, don't do a good job.

For most people, (a) is not an option. We simply don't have the time, desire, or ability to manage our own investments. Utilizing the simple and free strategy of Nest Egg Insurance, we can be assured that our hard-earned retirement money will be there for us when we reach retirement.

The good news is that this is not an "either/or" strategy. There is nothing to keep someone from having some of their retirement funds professionally managed with the hope of sky-high returns, while at the same time protecting a percentage of the nest egg with

Why Your Retirement Is at Risk

insurance so that 100 percent of your money is not at risk. Read the chapter on "The Rule of 100" for an easy rule of thumb that can get you started with this strategy.

At some point, everybody who has saved for retirement will have to come to the point where they switch gears and try to live off their nest egg. The key is to make it last for as long as you do. Since we do not know how long we will live, we have a dilemma. How do we make sure that we don't run out of money?

Financial experts will advise people to try to conserve their nest egg by taking out as small a percentage as possible. You will hear 4 percent as a typical number. This percentage will also roughly coincide with the federal government's mandate that at age 70½ you take required minimum distributions (RMDs) from qualified retirement plans. After all, Uncle Sam has let you delay paying taxes on all that money for your entire working life, and he wants to start collecting his share.

So here we have an interesting phenomenon. People who have had other people invest their money during their working lives are now faced with the prospect of managing that money so it will last as long as they live. Unfortunately, this phase often ends in disaster because many people are not self-disciplined enough to slowly draw down this money. A similar occurrence happens all the time with lottery winners.

People who have never had much in the way of financial assets are now faced with a large sum of money. We've all heard the stories of lottery winners who were broke in a matter of years. The problem is that they always seem to opt for the lump-sum payout (which, by itself, is not a bad choice if they can manage it properly) instead of a substantial annual income for the rest of their lives. So they pay a huge chunk in taxes (usually greater than 50 percent), take their big pile of cash, and spend like there's no tomorrow. A few years later, they're in the news because they're flat broke. Don't let this happen to you.

There have also been stories about people who got out before the dot-com bust and had several million dollars in retirement assets. One particular case was an Intel employee who had amassed close to $35 million! And yet, several years later this person was bankrupt. Remember, you can always spend more than you make (or have saved). Look at how much the federal government brings in, and they still spend more than they take in (it's called a deficit).

Give the federal government the Sahara Desert, and in five years we would have a shortage of sand.

So sometimes we need to realize that what we really need is protection from ourselves. Realizing that it is human nature to typically spend without regard for the future, we need to put safeguards in place so that all of our money is not available to us to spend at one time, so that we will have our money last as long as we do. Once someone wins the lottery, people come out of the woodwork trying to sell them something, have them "invest" in something, or borrow some money so that the cycle of riches to rags continues.

In order to keep this from happening, you not only have to be concerned with not spending at a pace that will eventually deplete your balance, but you also have to make sure that the balance will keep up with inflation and tax law changes. So how do you simultaneously make money while spending money? First, let's review how money is made.

It has been said that there are only two things that make money:

1. Money at work
2. People at work

The truth is, there is only one: people at work. Think about it. If you stick a pile of money in the middle of your living room, does it go to work? No. If you put it in a bank account, does it go to work? No. In order for money in a bank account to grow, people have to lend it out to someone who is willing to work hard and earn more than they borrowed in order to pay you a return on your money. So it is only people who make money by working. And you have to find people willing to work so that your money will grow. These people can be classified as either lenders (the return on the money is based on lending money in the form of debt that can be secured with collateral) or investors (where your money goes into a venture as a part owner and the return on your money is not guaranteed but has the *potential* for a greater return than secured debt).

Always remember the one indisputable law of money: the higher the return, the higher the risk; the lower the return, the lower the risk.

Nest egg insurance can accomplish this dual role of growth

DON'T BREAK MY NEST EGG

while producing an income stream to live off of. Take a look at the chart on the next page. Let's say you have a $200,000 nest egg. Simply put a portion, say roughly 25 percent, or $53,966, in a vehicle that pays out over a five-year period all the money plus interest. In effect, you have a reverse five-year loan. You pay in $53,966. You get paid back $1,000 per month for the next sixty months (five years) for a total of $60,000. At the end of the five years, your $53,966 is gone but the remaining $146,033 at an approximate yield of 7 percent has grown to $204,800 in nest egg insurance. Nest egg insurance has the added benefit of returning the majority of the money to you in a more tax efficient manner than living off the interest and paying taxes on 100 percent of the income you receive. In this instance, the $1,000 payout is approximately 90 percent tax-free, which, at the 28 percent tax bracket, provides for tax savings of $15,120. Combined with the 7 percent return on the deferred money, the benefit grows from $204,800 to $219,920! Then just repeat the process.

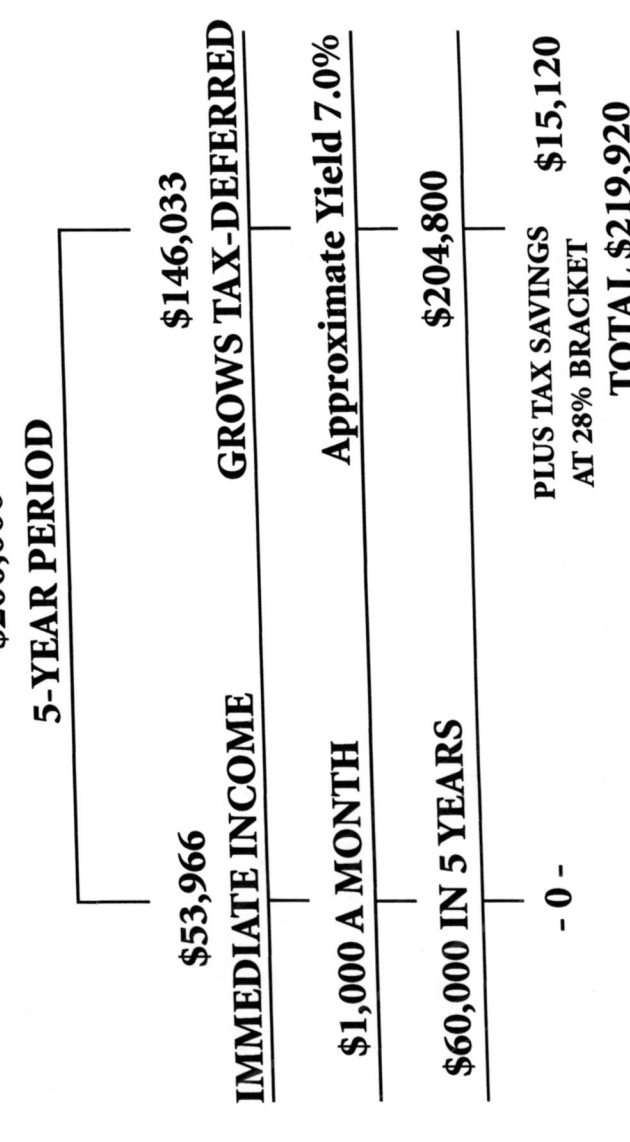

Guarantees are based on the claim's paying ability of the issuing insurance company. For illustrative purposes only—results may vary.

The Retirement Table of Doom

A LOT OF FINANCIAL EXPERTS WILL TRY TO SCARE THE PANTS OFF their clients by telling them they are going to have to get used to eating dog food during retirement. They pull out charts showing what inflation is going to do in the next thirty years, what their life expectancy is going to be, and that healthcare and prescription costs are going to deplete their retirement savings so that everybody will have to live in their vans down by the river and survive on nothing but government-subsidized cheese!

The presentation goes something like this: "You cannot count on Social Security or Medicare in retirement because those programs are going broke. Companies are ditching pension plans so you will be solely responsible for your own retirement. Let's say that you want to have a retirement income of $40,000. At a 4% withdrawal rate, that means you will need a nest egg of $1,000,000! Now let's review the following chart:"

The Retirement Table of Doom

Age	Amount
25	0
26	25,000
27	50,000
28	75,000
29	100,000
30	125,000
31	150,000
32	175,000
33	200,000
34	225,000
35	250,000
36	275,000
37	300,000
38	325,000
39	350,000
40	375,000
41	400,000
42	425,000
43	450,000
44	475,000
45	500,000
46	525,000
47	550,000
48	575,000
49	600,000
50	625,000
51	650,000

52	675,000
53	700,000
54	725,000
55	750,000
56	775,000
57	800,000
58	825,000
59	850,000
60	875,000
61	900,000
62	925,000
63	950,000
64	975,000
65	1,000,000

Having a retirement income of $40,000 per year . . .

living off 4 percent of your nest egg each year . . .

requires $1,000,000 by age sixty-five!

Look at your age and then see what you should have in your retirement account right now.

So, how are you doing?

DON'T BREAK MY NEST EGG

"If you wanted to retire at age sixty-five, and you started to save for retirement at age twenty-five, that would be forty years. If you divide the goal of $1,000,000 by forty years, you get $25,000 per year. So in order to see if you are going to reach your goal, let's take your age and compare it with how much money you should have in retirement savings at various stages in your life."

If you compare your own age to the balance you're supposed to have, you'll be able to see why I have labeled this the "Retirement Table of Doom."

Now I don't disagree with the math. It is what it is. The point I want to make is this: Wal-Mart sells millions of drills. A person who buys a drill wants a *hole*, not the drill. Utilizing this same line of reasoning, people need the *income* from their nest egg to live on in retirement. But it doesn't necessarily have to come from a big pile of cash.

And there are more ways than one to produce the $40,000 in retirement income. I highly recommend the book *Rich Dad, Poor Dad* by Robert Kiyosaki. There are several asset classes that can be utilized to produce income, not just one. He identifies three major asset classes people can use to produce an income stream.

They are:

1. *Paper Assets.* These are mutual funds, stocks, bonds, CDs, etc., the only asset class that financial advisers usually talk about. Why is that? Because these are the only things they are licensed to

sell and make a commission from. If you use any of your money to do the other two, they won't make any money!

2. *Real Estate Assets.* This is where people buy real estate as an investment, such as rental houses, apartments, and commercial property. Many people have retired with no substantial money in a retirement account because they have plenty of rental property to produce enough income to retire.

3. *Business Assets.* Many people are entrepreneurial and want to build equity in their own businesses. A properly run business can generate income even when the owner is not working in the business. Again, this asset class can produce an income stream sufficient to retire on as well.

If possible, and to also have a properly diversified income stream so that not all your income is dependent on one source, it would be preferable to have some income coming in from each of these three asset classes. People tend to get into big trouble when all their assets or all their income is in one basket, and then something bad happens to the basket.

We need to take personal responsibility and not blame others for our decision to put all our money into one asset class and let some stranger manage it. This is a recipe for a sad appearance on *60 Minutes!*

What this chart also shows is the problem the majority of Americans will face as they get older. There are really two big universal problems that have been identified as the reasons why many people will not have a comfortable retirement.

First people are not saving nearly enough for retirement. The vast majority of retirement accounts have less than $100,000 in them. In Stephen Covey's book *First Things First*, he talks about things that are important but not urgent. Almost universally, people will tell you that their retirement is important to them. However, there is no *urgency* because it seems so far away. Instead, we tend to spend most of our time dealing with things that are important and urgent (getting promoted at work) or unimportant and urgent (picking up dry cleaning), and by the time our retirement becomes both important *and* urgent, we find ourselves way behind the curve and we simply give up.

Second, people are not taking control of, or safeguarding their retirement assets. A lot of people invest either too conservatively (they get a very low rate of return by keeping their money in the bank) or very aggressively (they swing for a home run in the stock market and end up striking out instead). This is why a middle of the road strategy makes more sense for most people. Set aside a portion of your retirement money in nest egg insurance to protect it from loss, but this strategy will also allow it to participate in stock market gains without the risk.

If You Can't Afford to Lose It, Insure It!

That's the whole point. Why take the unnecessary risk, hoping that you retire before a market correction, when you can capture a good percentage of those gains without having to risk a major decline in your nest egg? If you were to go to Las Vegas and play blackjack, and the casino guaranteed that no matter how badly you played, they would at least give you back all the money you started with, how would you react to such a proposition? But the trade-off would be, instead of keeping 100 percent of your gains, you would have to share a percentage of your gains with the casino. Wouldn't you take them up on this offer?

Or how about this analogy: Remember the game show *The Weakest Link*? Contestants were asked a series of questions and, after every correct answer, they doubled their money. But if they answered incorrectly, they went back to zero. However, a contestant could "bank" their accumulated earnings at any time, and they would not risk losing what they had accumulated. They would have to start back at zero, but at least they would have had some money saved up if they lost that round or the entire game.

Many people continue to put all their retirement money at risk every day in the market. Some of these people might walk away from the game with very little. All because they would not "bank" some of their earnings along the way. They got greedy, and as a consequence they didn't get to keep all they had earned.

Think about it. A blue-chip stock like Merck lost *$30 billion* in market value in one day because they took Vioxx off the market. A terrorist attack like 9/11 would have a devastating effect on the market, and you have no control over such events. Why take the risk day in and day out when you have an attractive alternative?

The problem up to this point has been that you had no choice. You could choose between putting your money in the bank and getting a low rate of return, or putting it in the stock market to (ideally) get a higher rate of return along with the substantial risk of loss. Not the best trade-off.

People need a higher return than banks offer so they can keep up with inflation and not have to dip into their principal. Otherwise, in using this strategy you would run the risk of outliving your money. On the other hand, as you get older, you cannot afford to take any risk, since you don't have the time to recover from a major loss. Quite a predicament.

Now you don't have to make a choice between safety and returns. So how does this "nest egg insurance" work? How can an insurance company insure your nest egg, give you a 10 percent bonus on top of your contributions, give you a portion of the upside for greater returns, *and* guarantee that you will not lose any money? And oh, by the way, they also will not charge you any fees for providing this service! Sounds too good to be true? I'll explain.

The money you decide to insure with "nest egg insurance" will be placed with an insurance company. Your money is never at risk in the market. Rather, the returns are *linked* to one of several market indexes such as the S&P 500 or the NASDAQ 100, among others. The majority of your money is actually placed in high-grade government and corporate bonds. A portion of the money is used to purchase options on those indexes. Options give someone the right, but not the obligation, to buy something in the future.

For example, you could use an option to buy a house for a set price in the future. You would give the owner of the house a small payment for that right and then, if the house went up in value, you would have the option to purchase the house in the future for a price that had already been agreed on. If the house did not go up in value, you would lose what you paid for the option, but you would not have to go ahead with the purchase of the house. You have the right, but not the obligation.

So if the market indexes go up, the insurance company exercises the option, and depending on their crediting method (monthly, annually, average, point-to-point, etc.), you keep all of the gains up to a cap (maximum) or a participation rate (the percentage of the gain you get to keep). But if the market goes down, the company doesn't exercise the option, and there is no loss to be absorbed by you.

Here is an example of how one particular company credits your money based on one single year of using one of the most widely used market indexes, the S&P 500. This detail was for the year beginning 8/2/2004 and ending 8/1/2005. The S&P 500 returned 11.84 percent for the calendar year. If your money had been insured, your return would have been calculated using the following chart:

Policy Month	Actual S&P Index Gain (%)	or	Monthly Cap	=	Capped Monthly %
1	0.38%		3.3%		0.38%
2	2.31%		3.3%		2.31%
3	−0.09%		3.3%		−0.09%
4	5.38%		3.3%		3.30%
5	1.72%		3.3%		1.72%
6	−1.86%		3.3%		−1.86%
7	1.77%		3.3%		1.77%
8	−3.10%		3.3%		−3.10%
9	−1.37%		3.3%		−1.37%
10	3.92%		3.3%		3.30%
11	−0.65%		3.3%		−0.65%
12	3.43%		3.3%		3.30%

Total Return for the Year = 9.01%

The first thing you might notice is that the S&P went up by 11.84 percent, but you got to keep only 9.01 percent. That was more than one-third of the return! Not a good deal? Remember that these gains really aren't yours to keep unless you sell your shares and cash them in. That would be like buying a house in

Florida and then trying to predict ahead of time when the next hurricane was coming through and selling it before it hit. Good luck if you can accurately predict that in advance year after year.

The best news is that at least with this method, once you earn this return, it's yours to keep! You don't have to worry about figuring out when the market has peaked or having to sell your stocks so that you can cash in your gain. Every year, when this calculation is made, you will get any positive credit (up to a cap) that the particular market index returns. But if there is a negative return for the year, you will not take a loss. The insurance company will choose not to exercise the option, so there is no loss.

A secondary benefit is that when the market declines dramatically (as it did three years in a row from 2000 to 2002), you will not suffer any loss and, when the market does finally go up (as it did in 2003), you get to pick up the gains from where you left off. Everybody else will still be behind and trying to get back to even!

What recommendations do we give to people who are interested in "nest egg insurance"? First, just get started. It takes only $2,000 to open an account with retirement money ("qualified"), or $5,000 for non-retirement money ("nonqualified"). This money can be transferred from an existing bank or brokerage account. Then, as you get more information and comfort with this coverage, you can always move more money into the account at a later date.

If you are saving for retirement through work, for example with a 401(k) or 403(b) savings plan, keep doing it. Even though that money is not protected from a downturn in the market, many employers are matching a certain percentage of employee contributions. If you desire to save more money for retirement after you have reached the maximum employer match, then use any funds above this level to fund your "nest egg insurance." The insurance company will match your contributions by 10 percent, further increasing your retirement funds. And all of the funds put with the insurance company will be protected from a market decline.

You can open up an IRA, Roth IRA, Simplified Employee Pension (SEP), or Simple IRA with your nest egg insurance. You can roll over an old 401(k), IRA, or SEP into nest egg insurance. And you can continue to make contributions into your nest egg insurance by mailing in a check or having your checking account electronically debited. And remember, you will continue to get the 10 percent match on all deposits into your nest egg insurance.

Where can you purchase nest egg insurance?

First, check with your favorite financial adviser (if you have one). If they don't know about it or won't help you with it, you can contact us, and we will put you in touch with someone we recommend in your area.

You can reach us for additional information or help at:

www.nestegginsurance.com

If your insurance professional or financial adviser would like to find out more about nest egg insurance and how they could include selling it in their existing practice; or if you would like to join the cause by spreading the word to everyone with retirement assets to protect themselves with nest egg insurance, then go to this same Web site and request an orientation kit for insurance professionals.

We will be glad to educate them and help them get started so they can offer it to their clients at no cost or obligation.

Don't be like the unfortunate people who watched their retirement accounts drop by 50 percent or more just before they were preparing to retire. People back then did not have any choice. Nest egg insurance was not available to them, so they took the full brunt of the market storm. But it is available to you. Will you let this opportunity slip by because you don't believe it will happen to you, or your financial or other advisers tell you not to do it? Ask them to sign a guarantee in writing that will protect your retirement assets if they advise against it. And ask them for a copy of their E&O coverage (errors and omissions insurance). If they won't cooperate, you have your answer. They are not going to stand behind their recommendation. They just don't want to lose your business.

It's *your* money and *your* retirement. We're not advising that you move all your money into nest egg insurance. But you cannot afford to put 100 percent of your savings at risk. Social Security will not be enough to keep you financially secure if you are wrong. Insure at least a portion of your retirement savings. If the market continues to move up, you will still get the gains. If it goes down, you won't lose a dime. A win-win situation if there ever was one.

Finally, remember the retired couple at the beginning of this book. They had several opportunities to purchase insurance prior to losing their home to the hurricane. We don't pretend to know when or how severely the market may decline in the future. However, just like living on the coast of Florida, it's not a matter of "if" but "when."

It's not even a matter of whether or not a substantial decline will occur. The real question is, will you be prepared if it does?

One Final Question . . .

Would you be interested in a retirement savings vehicle that . . .

- ❑ pays up to a 10% bonus on every deposit you make

- ❑ is guaranteed not to lose money

- ❑ has the potential to return up to 32% a year in a strong bull market (2.7% per month maximum)

- ❑ charges no fees to your account

Then request more information at:

www.nestegginsurance.com

About the Author

DAVID VERNICH has more than twenty years experience in commercial lending, corporate cash management (attained the designation of Certified Cash Manager), individual insurance planning, and investments. He has earned a reputation of putting clients' interests first.

"My advice will stand the test of time," he asserts. "I can provide you with objective, independent feedback that will hold up in today's financial markets and tomorrow's too." He is a graduate (BA) of Ambassador College in Pasadena, California and has completed the MBA program at Tennessee State University in Nashville, Tennessee.

David combines a personal approach with the kind of openness, honesty and genuine concern for his clients' welfare that mark him as not just a reliable professional but as someone comfortable to work with.

For him the journey is as important as the destination, and his clients' long-range security is always reflected in their present-day comfort level.

David lives in Clarksville, Tennessee, with his wife, Connie, and their four sons.

Breinigsville, PA USA
12 August 2010
243484BV00001B/33/A